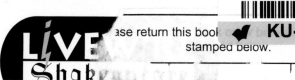

# William Shakespeare's

# Macbeth

EDITED BY

*Philip Page and Marilyn Pettit*

ILLUSTRATED BY

*Philip Page*

Published in association with

The
**Basic Skills**
Agency

Hodder & Stoughton

A MEMBER OF THE HODDER HEADLINE GROUP

Orders: please contact Bookpoint Ltd, 130 Milton Park, Abingdon, Oxon OX14 4SB.
Telephone: (44) 01235 827720, Fax: (44) 01235 400454. Lines are open from 9.00–6.00,
Monday to Saturday, with a 24 hour message answering service.
You can also order through our website www.hodderheadline.co.uk

*British Library Cataloguing in Publication Data*
A catalogue record for this title is available from The British Library

ISBN 0 340 74296 8

First published 1999
Impression number    10   9   8
Year                       2005   2004   2003

Cover illustration by Lee Stinton
Typeset by Fakenham Photosetting Ltd, Fakenham, Norfolk
Printed in Great Britain for Hodder & Stoughton Educational, a division of Hodder
Headline, 338 Euston Road, London NW1 3BH by J. W. Arrowsmith Ltd., Bristol.

# Contents

# About the play

*Macbeth* is a tragedy. Did you know that a tragedy has to follow rules?

It usually tells the story of a very important man or woman, who isn't as good as they should have been! He or she seems to start off well, but something happens – perhaps they make a mistake – and then things get worse and the character ends up in a terrible state, before dying.

No matter what happens, everyone knows that things will end badly in a tragedy.

Macbeth starts off as a very important man who has lots of good things in his life, but then something evil sets him thinking it could be even better. And when he shares his thoughts with his wife, there is no going back. He ends up killing more and more people, until he is forced to meet up with his worst enemy on the battlefield.

The play mostly takes place in the dark. It is violent and full of blood. As you read, make a note of how many times words to do with blood and the night are mentioned.

As you read, try to work out who Macbeth's worst enemy is – the one who finally kills him.

# Cast of characters

**Macbeth**
A brave soldier, who
becomes evil.

**Lady Macbeth**
An ambitious woman
who loves her husband.

**Duncan**
A Scottish king who gets
murdered.

**Malcolm**
Duncan's son who returns
from England to be king.

**Donalbain**
Malcolm's brother who
escapes to Ireland.

**Banquo**
Macbeth's friend who
becomes suspicious
and is murdered.

**Fleance**
Banquo's son who
escapes death.

**Macduff**
A brave Scottish
thane (nobleman).

**Lady Macduff**
Macduff's wife
who is murdered.

**Lenox**
A Scottish nobleman.

**Ross**
A Scottish nobleman.

**Seyton**
Macbeth's servant.

**Doctor**
Works in Macbeth's castle.
Fails to cure Lady Macbeth.

**Siward**
A soldier who fights for
Malcolm against Macbeth.

**Young Siward**
Siward's son who is
killed by Macbeth.

**Three Witches**
Evil spirits who cause
trouble for Macbeth.

**Hecate**
The Goddess of the
Witches.

Three witches appear in a storm and talk about their next meeting!

When shall we three meet again?
In thunder, lightning, or in rain?

When the **hurlyburly's** done,
When the battle's lost and won.

That will be **ere** the set of sun.

Where the place?

Upon the heath.

There to meet with Macbeth.

**hurlyburly** – fighting     **ere** – before

## Think about it

What do you think 'Fair is foul and foul is fair' might mean?

We hear the name Macbeth — what might we be wondering?

**Greymalkin** – a grey cat    **Paddock** – a toad

| Act 1 Scene 2 | King Duncan is too old to fight. A soldier tells him about the battle and Macbeth's bravery. |

What bloody man is that?

This is the sergeant who fought 'gainst my captivity.

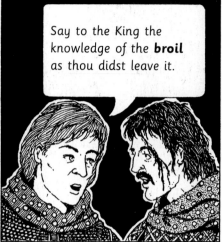

Say to the King the knowledge of the **broil** as thou didst leave it.

Doubtful it stood; as two spent swimmers, that do cling together and choke their art. But all's too weak, for brave Macbeth with his **brandish'd steel**, which smok'd with bloody execution, like **Valour's minion**, carv'd out his passage till he fac'd **the slave**.

He unseam'd him from the nave to the chaps, and fix'd his head upon our battlements.

O valiant cousin! Worthy gentleman!

**broil** – fighting    **brandish'd steel** – sword
**Valour's minion** – courage's friend    **the slave** – the rebel leader

3

**Bellona's bridegroom** – the husband of the Goddess of War

| Act 1 Scene 3 | Macbeth and Banquo return from fighting. They meet the Three Witches who make some predictions . . . |

**attire** – clothes

**Macbeth:** So foul and fair a day I have not seen.

[*The Three Witches appear*]

**Banquo:** What are these,
So withered and so wild in their **attire**,
That look not like th' inhabitants o' th' earth,
And yet are on't? Live you? Or are you aught
That man may question? You seem to understand me,
By each at once her choppy finger laying
Upon her skinny lips; you should be women,
And yet your beards forbid me to interpret
That you are so.

**Macbeth:** Speak, if you can. What are you?

**First Witch:** All hail, Macbeth! hail to thee,
Thane of Glamis!

**Second Witch:** All hail, Macbeth! hail to thee,
Thane of Cawdor!

**Third Witch:** All hail, Macbeth!
that shalt be king hereafter!

**Banquo:** Good sir, why do you start and seem to fear
Things that do sound so fair?
My noble partner you greet with present grace
And great prediction of noble having, and of royal hope,
That he seems **rapt withal**; to me you speak not.
If you can look into the seeds of time,
And say which grain will grow, and which will not,
Speak then to me, who neither beg, nor fear,
Your favours nor your hate.

**rapt withal** – in a daze

**First Witch:** Lesser than Macbeth, and greater.

**Second Witch:** Not so happy, yet much happier.

**Third Witch:** Thou shalt get kings, though thou be none:
So all hail, Macbeth and Banquo!

**Macbeth:** Stay, you imperfect speakers, tell me more.
By Sinel's death I know I am Thane of Glamis;
But how of Cawdor? The Thane of Cawdor lives,
A prosperous gentleman; and to be King
Stands not within the prospect of belief,
No more than to be Cawdor.

[*The Witches vanish*]

**Banquo:** The earth hath bubbles, as the water has,
And these are of them. Whither are they vanish'd?

**Macbeth:** Into the air. Would they had stay'd!

**Banquo:** Were such things here, as we do speak about,
Or have we eaten on the **insane root**,
That takes the reason prisoner?

**insane root** – a plant that could make you mad

**Macbeth:** Your children shall be kings.

**Banquo:** You shall be King.

**Macbeth:** And Thane of Cawdor too; went it not so?

**Banquo:** To th'selfsame tune, and words. Who's here?

---

**Think about it**

Where have you heard 'foul and fair' before?

What does this suggest to you?

---

**Act 1 Scene 3**

Macbeth finds out that the Witches have told him truth! What next?

The King hath happily receiv'd, Macbeth, the news of thy success. He bade me, from him, call thee Thane of Cawdor.

What! can the Devil speak true!

The Thane of Cawdor lives: why do you dress me in borrow'd robes?

Who was the Thane lives yet, but under heavy judgment bears that life which he deserves to lose.

Glamis and Thane of Cawdor: the greatest is behind.

Do you not hope your children shall be kings?

'Tis strange: and oftentimes, to win us to our harm, the instruments of Darkness tell us truths; win us with honest **trifles**, to betray us.

**trifles** – small, worthless things

This **supernatural soliciting** cannot be ill; cannot be good: if ill, why hath it given me earnest of success, commencing in a truth? I am Thane of Cawdor.

If good, why do I yield to that suggestion whose horrid image doth unfix my hair and make my seated heart knock at my ribs against the use of nature?

Look how our partner's rapt.

If chance will have me king, why, chance may crown me without my stir.

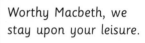

Worthy Macbeth, we stay upon your leisure.

Give me your favour, my dull brain was wrought with things forgotten. Come, friends.

### Think about it

Look at the way Macbeth and Banquo act in this scene. What does this tell you about the two men?

**supernatural soliciting** – the Witches' greetings

Duncan is pleased to see Macbeth. He will stay with Macbeth at his castle. But ... he says that his son, Malcolm, will be king after him!

Is execution done on Cawdor?

He was a gentleman on whom I built an absolute trust.

O worthiest cousin! **More is thy due than more than all can pay**.

Sons, kinsmen, Thanes, know we will establish our estate upon our eldest, Malcolm; whom we name the Prince of Cumberland.

From hence to Inverness, and bind us further to you.

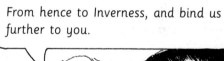

I'll myself be the **harbinger**, and make joyful the hearing of my wife with your approach.

The Prince of Cumberland! That is a step on which I must fall down, or else o'erleap for in my way it lies.

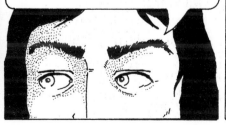

**Think about it**

What do these last words of Macbeth tell us about his thoughts?

**More is thy due ...** – I owe you more than I can give        **harbinger** – messenger

9

| Act 1 Scene 5 | Lady Macbeth has read a letter from her husband telling her what the Witches said. She decides that Duncan will have to be killed. |
| --- | --- |

**Lady Macbeth:** Glamis thou art, and Cawdor; and shalt be
What thou art promis'd. Yet do I fear thy nature:
It is too full o' th' milk of human kindness,
To catch the nearest way. Thou wouldst be great;
Art not without ambition, but without
The illness should attend it. Hie thee hither
That I may pour my spirits into thine ear,
And chastise thee with the valour of my tongue
All that impedes thee from **the golden round**.                    the crown
                    [*A messenger arrives*]
What is your tidings?

**Messenger:** The King comes here tonight.

**Lady Macbeth:** Thou'rt mad to say it.
Is not thy master with him?

**Messenger:** Our Thane is coming;
One of my fellows had the speed of him.

**Lady Macbeth:** Give him tending: he brings great news.
                    [*The messenger leaves*]
The raven himself is hoarse,
That croaks the fatal entrance of Duncan
Under my battlements. Come, you Spirits
That tend on mortal thoughts, unsex me here,
And fill me, from the crown to the toe, top-full
Of direst cruelty! Come to my woman's breasts,
And take my milk for gall, you murdering ministers!
Come, thick night,
And **pall** thee in the **dunnest** smoke of Hell,          **pall** – to wrap up a dead body
That my keen knife see not the wound it makes,              **dunnest** – darkest
Nor Heaven peep through the blanket of the dark,
To cry, 'Hold, hold!'

                    [*Macbeth enters*]

**Macbeth:** My dearest love,
Duncan comes here tonight.

**Lady Macbeth:** And when goes hence?

**Macbeth:** Tomorrow, as he **purposes**.          intends

**Lady Macbeth:** O! never shall sun that morrow see!
Your face, my Thane, is as a book, where men
May read strange matters. To **beguile the time**,          trick everybody
Look like the time; bear welcome in your eye,
Your hand, your tongue: look like th'innocent flower,
But be the serpent under't. He that's coming
Must be provided for; and you shall put
This night's great business **into my dispatch**.          leave it to me

---

**Think about it**

What does Lady Macbeth think of her husband?

What kind of woman is Lady Macbeth?

What do you make of the line:
'He that's coming
Must be provided for;'?

---

Duncan arrives at the Macbeth's castle. He likes it and is happy to be their guest for the night.

This castle hath a pleasant seat: the air nimbly and sweetly recommends itself unto our senses.

The temple haunting **martlet**, does approve, by his loved mansionry, that the heaven's breath smells wooingly here.

See our honoured hostess.

All our service, in every point twice done, and then done double, were poor against those honours wherewith Your Majesty loads our house.

Fair and noble hostess, we are your guest tonight.

At your Highness's pleasure.

### Think about it

What do we know at this point that makes us feel worried for Duncan?

What do you think of Lady Macbeth's behaviour?

**martlet** – a bird that nests in buildings

| **Act 1 Scene 7** | Macbeth thinks about killing Duncan. He has arguments for and against, but mostly against! |
|---|---|

If it were done, when 'tis done, then 'twere well it were done quickly.

That but this blow might be the be-all and the end-all – here, we'd jump the life to come.

But in these cases we still have judgment here.

He's here in double trust: first as I am his kinsman and his subject.

Then, as his host, who should against his murderer shut the door, not bear the knife myself.

Besides, this Duncan hath borne his faculties so meek, hath been so clear in his great office.

I have no spur to prick the sides of my intent, but only vaulting ambition.

Lady Macbeth persuades Macbeth to murder Duncan. She mocks him; she tells him her plan and he agrees to do the deed.

**Macbeth:** We will proceed no further in this business:
He hath honour'd me of late; and I have bought
Golden opinions from all sorts of people.

**Lady Macbeth:** Was the hope drunk
Wherein you dress'd yourself? Hath it slept since?
And wakes it now, to look so green and pale
At what it did so freely? From this time
Such I account thy love. Would'st thou have that
Which thou esteem'st **the ornament of life**,          the crown
And live a coward in thine own esteem,
Letting 'I dare not' wait upon 'I would,'
Like the poor **cat i'th'adage**?          A cat in a story who wanted fish but was afraid to get his paws wet.

**Macbeth:** I dare do all that may become a man;
Who dares do more, is none.

**Lady Macbeth:** What beast was't then
That made you break this enterprise to me?
When you durst do it, then you were a man.
Nor time, nor place,
Did then adhere, and yet you would make both:
They have made themselves now, and that their fitness now
Does unmake you. I have given suck, and know
How tender 'tis to love the babe that milks me:
I would, while it was smiling in my face,
Have pluck'd my nipple from his boneless gums,
**And dash'd the brains out, had I so sworn**          Lady Macbeth would have killed her
**As you have done to this.**          baby if she had sworn to do it, in the same way Macbeth has sworn to murder Duncan.

**Macbeth:** If we should fail?

**Lady Macbeth:** We fail?
But screw your courage to the sticking-place,
And we'll not fail. When Duncan is asleep
His two **chamberlains** will I with wine and **wassail** so convince,
That memory, the warder of the brain,
Shall be a fume, and the receipt of reason
A **limbeck** only: when in swinish sleep
Their drenched nature lie, as in a death,
What cannot you and I perform upon
Th'unguarded Duncan? what not put upon
His **spongy** officers, who shall bear the guilt
Of our great **quell**?

**chamberlains** – guards
**wassail** – merry-making

**limbeck** – jar or flask

**spongy** – drunken
**quell** – murder

**Macbeth: Bring forth men-children only!**
Will it not be receiv'd,
When we have mark'd with blood those sleepy two
Of his own chamber, and us'd their very daggers,
That they have done't?

because men are supposed to be
tougher than women

**Lady Macbeth:** Who dares receive it other,
As we shall make our griefs and clamour roar
Upon his death?

**Macbeth:** I am settled, and bend up
Each corporal agent to this terrible feat.
Away, and mock the time with fairest show:
False face must hide what the false heart doth know.

---

**Think about it**

Who would you say is the stronger character?

---

| **Act 2 Scene 1** | It is night. Banquo and Macbeth talk. Macbeth pretends he hasn't thought about the Witches, but he suggests that they have a chat about them later on! |

Give me my sword. Who's there.

A friend.

All's well. I dreamt last night of the three Weird Sisters: to you they have show'd some truth.

I think not of them.

Yet, when we can entreat an hour to serve, we would spend it in some words upon that business.

At your kind'st leisure.

If you shall cleave to my consent, when 'tis, it shall make honour for you.

So I lose none in seeking to augment it.

Good repose, the while!

Thanks, Sir: the like to you.

### Think about it

Banquo should feel safe in Macbeth's castle, but he jumps when Macbeth comes along. What do you think of this?

| **Act 2 Scene 1** | Macbeth waits for the signal from his wife that Duncan's guards are asleep. He imagines that he sees a dagger leading the way to Duncan's room. |
| --- | --- |

Go bid thy mistress, when my drink is ready, she strike upon the bell.

Is this a dagger, which I see before me, the handle toward my hand?

I have thee not and yet I see thee still.

Thou marshall'st me the way that I was going.

And on thy blade and **dudgeon**, **gouts** of blood which was not so before.

There's no such thing. It is the bloody business which informs thus to mine eyes.

Thou sure and firm-set earth, hear not my steps.

The bell invites me.

Hear it not, Duncan; for it is a knell that summons thee to Heaven, or to Hell.

**dudgeon** – handle    **gouts** – drops

<table>
<tr><td>**Act 2**<br>**Scene 2**</td><td>Macbeth has killed Duncan, but already he is sorry. He messes up the plan and Lady Macbeth has to sort things out.</td></tr>
</table>

**Lady Macbeth:** I laid their daggers ready;
He could not miss 'em. Had he not resembled
My father as he slept, I had done't.

> [*Enter Macbeth*]

**Macbeth:** I have done the deed. Did'st thou not hear a noise?

**Lady Macbeth:** I heard the owl scream and the crickets cry.

**Macbeth:** This is a sorry sight.

**Lady Macbeth:** A foolish thought to say a sorry sight.

**Macbeth:** There's one did laugh in's sleep and one cried
'Murder!'
That they did wake each other: I stood and heard them;
But they did say their prayers. I could not say 'Amen'
When they did say, 'God bless us.'

**Lady Macbeth:** Consider it not so deeply.

**Macbeth:** But wherefore could I not pronounce 'Amen'?
I had most need of blessing, and 'Amen' stuck in my throat.

**Lady Macbeth:** These deeds must not be thought
After these ways: so, it will make us mad.

**Macbeth:** Methought, I heard a voice cry, 'Sleep no more!
Macbeth doth murder sleep'.

**Lady Macbeth:** Who was it thus cried? Why, worthy Thane,
You do unbend your noble strength, to think
So brainsickly of things. Go, get some water,
And wash this filthy witness from your hand.
Why did you bring these daggers from the place?
They must lie there: go, carry them, and smear
The sleepy grooms with blood.

**Macbeth:** I'll go no more:
I am afraid to think what I have done;
Look on't again I dare not.

**Lady Macbeth: Infirm of purpose!**                    useless!
Give me the daggers. The sleeping, and the dead,
Are but as pictures; 'tis the eye of childhood
That fears a painted devil. If he do bleed,
I'll gild the faces of the grooms withal,
For it must seem their guilt.

[*Lady Macbeth leaves*]

**Macbeth:** Whence is that knocking?
How is't with me, when every noise appals me?
Will all great Neptune's ocean wash this blood
Clean from my hand? No, this my hand will rather
The multitudinous seas **incarnadine**                    blood-red dye
Making the green one red.

[*Lady Macbeth returns*]

**Lady Macbeth:** My hands are of your colour; but I shame
To wear a heart so white. I hear a knocking
At the south entry: retire we to our chamber.
A little water clears us of this deed:
How easy is it then?
Get on your night-gown, lest occasion call us,
And show us to be watchers. Be not lost
So poorly in your thoughts.

**Macbeth:** To know my deed, 'twere best not to know myself.
Wake Duncan with thy knocking: I would thou could'st!

---

### Think about it

Is Lady Macbeth still the stronger character?

What has worried Macbeth?

---

Duncan's body is found. The men must meet to work out what to do next. Duncan's sons are scared – they decide to run off.

Is the King stirring?

Not yet.

I'll make so bold to call.

Awake! awake! Ring the alarum-bell. Murder and treason!

What's the business?

O gentle lady, 'tis not for you to hear what I can speak.

O Banquo! Our royal master's murdered!

Woe, alas! What! in our house?

Too cruel anywhere.

Your royal father's murder'd!

By whom?

Those of his chamber, as it seem'd, had done't. Their hands and faces were all badg'd with blood.

O! yet I do repent me of my fury that I did kill them.

Wherefore did you so?

Here lay Duncan, his silver skin lac'd with his golden blood: there the murderers, their daggers unmannerly breech'd with gore.

Who could refrain?

Help me!

Look to the lady.

Let us meet and question this most bloody piece of work.

What will you do? I'll to England.

To Ireland, I: where we are, there's daggers in men's smiles.

### Think about it

Macbeth has destroyed evidence. Why does he say he has done this?

Why does Lady Macbeth faint?

| **Act 2 Scene 4** | After Duncan's murder, strange things happen in the country. |  |

**Old Man: Threescore and ten** I can remember well;
Within the volume of which time I have seen
Hours dreadful, and things strange, but this sore night
Hath trifled former knowings.

70 years

**Ross:** Ha, good Father, by th'clock 'tis day,
And yet dark night strangles **the travelling lamp**.
Is't night's predominance, or the day's shame,
That darkness does the face of earth entomb,
When living light should kiss it?

the sun

**Old Man:** 'Tis unnatural,
Even like the deed's that done. On Tuesday last,
A falcon, towering in her pride of place,
Was by a mousing owl hawk'd at, and kill'd.

**Ross:** And Duncan's horses (a thing most strange and certain)
Beauteous and swift, **the minions** of their race,
Turn'd wild in nature, broke their stalls, flung out,
Contending 'gainst obedience, as they would make
War with mankind.

the very best

**Old Man:** 'Tis said, they ate each other.

**Ross:** They did so; to th'amazement of mine eyes,
That look'd upon't. Here comes the good Macduff.

---

### Think about it

Why do you think all these strange things happen?

Could it be anything to do with Duncan being a king?

---

Ross and Macduff talk about the murder. Macduff tells Ross that Macbeth is about to be crowned King of Scotland.

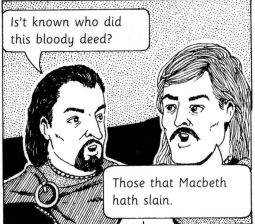

Is't known who did this bloody deed?

Those that Macbeth hath slain.

What good could they **pretend**?

They were **suborn'd**. The King's two sons are stol'n away and fled, which puts upon them suspicion of the deed.

Then 'tis most like the sovereignty will fall upon Macbeth.

He is already nam'd, and gone to Scone to be invested.

Where is Duncan's body?

Carried to Colme-kill.

Will you to Scone?

No cousin; I'll to Fife.

Well, I will thither.

Well, may you see things well done there. Lest our old robes sit easier than our new!

## Think about it

Do you notice anything about the way Macduff answers Ross?

**pretend** – intend     **suborn'd** – bribed

23

| Act 3 Scene 1 | Banquo suspects that Macbeth murdered Duncan. Macbeth does not trust Banquo and remembers what the Witches said about Banquo. |  |
| --- | --- | --- |

**Banquo:**  Thou hast it now, King, Cawdor, Glamis, all,
As the Weird Women promis'd; and, I fear,
Thou play'dst most foully for't; yet it was said,
It should not stand in thy posterity;
But that myself should be the root and father
Of many kings.

[*Enter Macbeth and Lady Macbeth*]

**Macbeth:**  Tonight we hold a solemn supper, Sir,
And I'll request your presence.

**Banquo:**  Let Your Highness
Command upon me, to the which my duties
Are with a most indissoluble tie
For ever knit.

**Macbeth:**  Ride you this afternoon?

**Banquo:**  Ay, my good Lord.

**Macbeth:**  Is't far you ride?

**Banquo:**  As far, my Lord, as will fill up the time
'Twixt this and supper.

**Macbeth:**  Goes Fleance with you?

**Banquo:**  Ay, my good Lord; our time does call upon's.

**Macbeth:**  I wish your horses swift, and sure of foot;
Farewell.

[*Banquo leaves*]

Let every man be master of his time
Till seven at night;
To make society the sweeter welcome,
We will keep ourselves till supper-time alone:
While then, God be with you.

*[Everybody else leaves]*

To be thus is nothing, but to be safely thus:
Our fears in Banquo
Stick deep, and in his royalty of nature
Reigns that which would be fear'd: 'tis much he dares;
And to that **dauntless temper** of his mind,          noble quality
He hath a wisdom that doth guide his valour
To act in safety. There is none but he
Whose being I do fear. He chid the Sisters,
When first they put the name of King upon me,
And bade them speak to him; then, prophet-like,
They hail'd him father to a line of kings:
Upon my head they plac'd **a fruitless crown**.          } Macbeth will have no children to
And put **a barren sceptre** in my gripe,          } follow him
No son of mine succeeding. If't be so,
For Banquo's issue have I fil'd my mind;
For them the gracious Duncan have I murder'd;
To make them kings, the seed of Banquo kings!

---

**Think about it**

What is really bothering Macbeth?

Why does he check on Banquo's plans for that afternoon?

Both of you know, Banquo was your enemy.

True, my Lord.

So is he mine; and thence it is that I to your assistance do make love.

We shall, my Lord, perform what you command us.

I will advise you where to plant yourselves, for't must be done to-night.

Fleance his son, that keeps him company, must embrace the fate of that dark hour.

It is concluded: Banquo, thy soul's flight, if it find Heaven, must find it out to-night.

We are resolv'd my Lord.

<table>
<tr><td>

**Act 3
Scene 2**

</td><td>

Lady Macbeth is worried about her husband. They aren't sleeping well, but Macbeth tells her that he has arranged something. However, he won't tell her what it is yet!

</td><td></td></tr>
</table>

**Lady Macbeth:** Nought's had, all's spent,
Where our desire is got without content:
'Tis safer to be that which we destroy,
Than by destruction dwell in doubtful joy.
How now, my Lord? Why do you keep alone,
Using those thoughts, which should indeed have died
With them they think on? What's done is done.

**Macbeth:** We have scorch'd the snake, not kill'd it:    We are still threatened
She'll close and be herself; whilst our poor malice
Remains in danger of her former tooth.
But let **the frame of things disjoint**, both the worlds suffer,    the universe fall apart
Ere we will eat our meal in fear, and sleep
In the affliction of these terrible dreams,
That shake us nightly. Better be with the dead,
Whom we, to gain our peace, have sent to peace,
Than on the torture of the mind to lie
In restless ecstasy. Duncan is in his grave;
Nothing can touch him further!

**Lady Macbeth:** Gentle my Lord, sleek o'er your rugged looks;
Be bright and jovial among your guests tonight.

**Macbeth:** So shall I, Love; and so, I pray, be you.
Let your remembrance apply to Banquo:
Present him eminence, both with eye and tongue:
And make our faces **vizards** to our hearts,    masks
Disguising what they are.

**Lady Macbeth:** You must leave this.

**Macbeth:** O! full of scorpions is my mind, dear wife!
Thou know'st that Banquo, and his Fleance, lives.

**Lady Macbeth:** But in them Nature's copy's not eterne.

**Macbeth:** There's comfort yet; they are assailable;
Then be thou **jocund**. Ere the bat hath flown                    happy
His cloister'd flight, there shall be done
A deed of dreadful note.

**Lady Macbeth:** What's to be done?

**Macbeth:** Be innocent of the knowledge, **dearest chuck,**      dear, sweetheart
Till thou applaud the deed. Come seeling Night,
Scarf up the tender eye of pitiful Day,
And, with thy bloody and invisible hand,
Cancel, and tear to pieces, that great bond
Which keeps me pale! Light thickens; and the crow
Makes wing to th'rooky wood;
Good things of Day begin to droop and drowse,
Whiles Night's black agents to their prey's do rouse.
Thou marvell'st at my words: but hold thee still;
Things bad begun make strong themselves by ill.

---

### Think about it

Why does Macbeth keep his plans for Banquo
and Fleance from Lady Macbeth?

---

<table>
<tr><td>**Act 3<br>Scene 3**</td><td>The murderers lie in wait for Banquo and Fleance. They attack, but their plan goes wrong!</td></tr>
</table>

But who did bid thee join us?

Macbeth.

He needs not our mistrust.

Stand with us. The west yet glimmers with some streaks of day.

Hark! I hear horses.

Then 'tis he: the rest are already i' th' court.

It will be rain tonight.

Let it come down!

Treachery! Fly, good Fleance, fly!

The son is fled.

We have lost best half of our affair.

Well, let's away and say how much is done.

At the banquet, Macbeth finds out that Banquo has been killed, but Fleance has escaped.

You know your own degrees, sit down: at first and last, the hearty welcome.

To all our friends; they are welcome.

There's blood upon thy face.

'Tis Banquo's, then.

Is he dispatch'd?

My Lord, his throat is cut. That I did for him.

He's good that did the like for Fleance.

Most royal Sir . . . Fleance is scap'd.

Then comes my fit again: I had else been perfect.

<table>
<tr><td>**Act 3<br>Scene 4**</td><td>Banquo's ghost appears. Macbeth loses control of himself and almost gives the game away. Lady Macbeth has to make excuses for him.</td></tr>
</table>

**Lady Macbeth:** My royal Lord, you do not give the cheer.

**Macbeth:** Sweet **remembrancer**.
Now, good digestion wait on appetite,
And health on both!

      [*Banquo's ghost appears and sits in Macbeth's place*]

someone who reminds someone of something

**Ross:** Please't your Highness to grace us with your royal company?

**Macbeth:** The table's full.

**Lenox:** Here is a place reserv'd, Sir.

**Macbeth:** Which of you have done this?
Thou can'st not say I did it: never shake
Thy **gory** locks at me.

bloody

**Ross:** His Highness is not well.

**Lady Macbeth:** Sit, worthy friends. My Lord is often thus.
The fit is momentary. Feed, and regard him not.
[*To Macbeth*] Are you a man?

**Macbeth:** Ay, and a bold one, that dare look on that.

**Lady Macbeth:** O proper stuff! This is the very painting of
your fear:
This is the air-drawn dagger, which, you said,
Led you to Duncan.
Why do you make such faces? When all's done,
You look but on a stool.

**Macbeth:** Prithee, see there!
If you can'st nod, speak too,
If **charnel-houses** and our graves must send
Those we bury back, our monuments
Shall be the **maws of kites**.  [*The ghost disappears*]

places where corpses are placed

stomachs of kites (flesh-eating birds)

31

**Lady Macbeth:**  What! quite unmann'd in folly?

**Macbeth:**  If I stand here, I saw him. The time has been,
That, when the brains were out, the man would die,
And there an end; but now, they rise again,
With twenty mortal murders on their crowns,
And push us from our stools.

**Lady Macbeth:**  My worthy Lord, your noble friends do
lack you.

**Macbeth:**  Do not muse at me, my most worthy friends,
I have a strange **infirmity**, which is nothing          illness
To those that know me. Come, love and health to all;
And to our dear friend Banquo, whom we miss.
                              [*The ghost reappears*]
**Avaunt!** And quit my sight! Let the earth hide thee!          Go away!
Thy bones are marrowless, thy blood is cold.

**Lady Macbeth:**  Think of this, good peers,
But as a thing of custom: 'tis no other.

**Macbeth:**  Take any shape but that, and my firm nerves
Shall never tremble. Hence, horrible shadow!
                              [*The ghost disappears*]
I am a man again. Pray you, sit still.

**Lady Macbeth:**  You have **displac'd the mirth**, broke the          spoilt the mood
good meeting
With most admir'd disorder.

**Macbeth:**  Can such things be,
When now I think you can behold such sights,
And keep the natural ruby of your cheeks,
When mine is blanch'd with fear?

**Ross:**  What sights, my Lord?

**Lady Macbeth:**  I pray you, speak not;
But go at once.

---

### Think about it

What must Ross, Lenox and the other noblemen of Scotland think now?

Does Lady Macbeth realise what is happening?

When the guests have left, Macbeth tells his wife that he will go to see the Witches. He wants to know what will happen next.

It will have blood, they say: blood will have blood: stones have been known to move, and trees to speak.

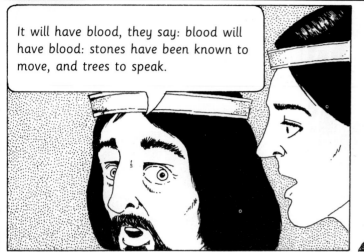

How say'st thou, that Macduff denies his person at our great bidding?

Did you send to him, Sir?

I heard it by the way, but I will send.

There's not a one of them, but in his house I keep **a servant fee'd**.

I will tomorrow to the Weird Sisters: more shall they speak; for now I am bent to know the worst for mine own good.

I am in blood stepp'd in so far, that, should I wade no more, returning were as tedious as go o'er.

You lack the season of all natures, sleep.

Come, we'll to sleep. We are yet but young in deed.

**a servant fee'd** – a paid spy

33

Hecate, the Goddess of Witches, is angry! She tells the Three Witches off for speaking to Macbeth.

Why, how now, Hecate? You look angerly.

Have I not reason? How did you dare to trade and traffic with Macbeth, in riddles, and affairs of death; and I was never call'd to bear my part, or show the glory of our art.

And, which is worse, all you have done hath been but for a wayward son, who loves for his own ends, not for you.

Meet me i' th' morning: thither he will come to know his destiny.

He shall spurn fate, scorn death, and bear his hopes 'bove wisdom, grace, and fear.

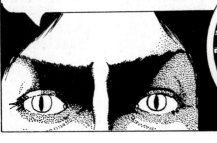

Hark! I am call'd.

Come, let's make haste: she'll soon be back again.

Lenox and another Scottish lord talk. We find out that Macduff is in England trying to get help to fight against Macbeth.

I hear Macduff lives in disgrace. Can you tell me where he bestows himself?

The son of Duncan lives in the English court.

Thither Macduff is gone to pray **the holy King**, upon his aid to wake Northumberland, and war-like Siward.

By the help of these, we may again give to our tables meat, sleep to our nights, free from our feasts and banquets bloody knives, do faithful homage, and receive free honours, all which we pine for now.

This report hath so exasperate **the King** that he prepares for war.

Sent he to Macduff?

He did: and with an absolute 'Sir, not I,' the messenger turns me his back.

**the holy King** – King Edward of England    **the King** – Macbeth

35

Macbeth visits the Witches. They show him spirits that make him feel safe. He only gets mad when he sees Banquo's sons as kings.

Double, double toil and trouble: fire burn and cauldron bubble.

By the pricking of my thumbs, something wicked this way comes.

How now, you secret, black, and midnight hags! What is't you do?

A deed without a name.

I conjure you, by that which you profess, howe'er you come to know it, answer me.

Speak. Demand. We'll answer.

Say if thou'dst rather hear it from our mouths, or from our masters?

Call 'em; let me see 'em.

Macbeth! beware Macduff; beware the Thane of Fife.

For thy good caution, thanks.

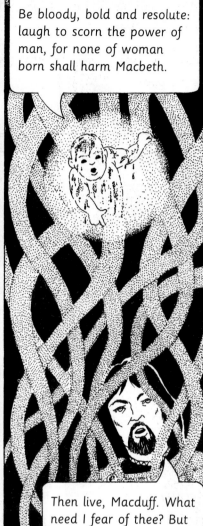

Be bloody, bold and resolute: laugh to scorn the power of man, for none of woman born shall harm Macbeth.

Then live, Macduff. What need I fear of thee? But yet thou shalt not live.

Macbeth shall never vanquish'd be, until Great Birnam wood to high Dunsinane hill shall come against him.

That will never be.

Shall Banquo's **issue** ever reign in this kingdom?

issue – son

Seek to know no more.

Deny me this, and an eternal curse fall on you!

Show his eyes and grieve his heart.

Filthy hags! Why do you show me this? Banquo smiles upon me, and points at them for his.

Where are they?

Saw you the Weird Sisters?

No, my Lord.

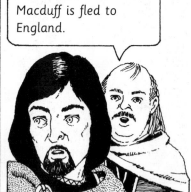

Macduff is fled to England.

The castle of Macduff I will surprise; seize upon Fife; give to th' edge o' th' sword his wife, his babes, and all unfortunate souls that trace him in his line.

Lady Macduff cannot understand why her husband has left his family to go to England. She is warned that she is in danger, but she cannot escape Macbeth's murderers.

What had he done, to make him fly the land?

You know not whether it was his wisdom, or his fear.

Wisdom! to leave his wife, to leave his babes?

I am so much a fool, should I stay longer. I take my leave at once.

After Ross leaves, a messenger comes to warn Lady Macduff that she is in danger.

Be not found here; hence, with your little ones. I dare abide no longer.

Whither should I fly? I have done no harm.

Where is your husband?

I hope, in no place so unsanctified, where such as thou may'st find him.

<table>
<tr><td>Act 4<br>Scene 3</td><td>In England Macduff meets Malcolm to try to persuade him to save Scotland. Malcolm has to test Macduff first.</td><td></td></tr>
</table>

**Malcolm:** I think our country sinks beneath the yoke;
It weeps, it bleeds; and each new day a gash
Is added to her wounds. From gracious England have I offer
Of goodly thousands: but, for all this,
When I shall tread upon the tyrant's head,
Or wear it on my sword, yet my poor country
Shall have more vices than it had before,
More suffer, and more sundry ways than ever,
By him that shall succeed.

**Macduff:** What should he be?

**Malcolm:** It is myself I mean; in whom I know
All the particulars of vice so grafted,
That, when they shall be open'd, black Macbeth
Will seem as pure as snow.

**Macduff:** Not in the legions
Of horrid Hell can come a devil more damn'd
In evils to top Macbeth.

**Malcolm:** I grant him bloody,
Luxurious, **avaricious**, false, deceitful,                          greedy
Sudden, malicious, smacking of every sin
That has a name; but there's no bottom, none,
In my voluptuousness: better Macbeth,
Than such a one to reign. Were I king,
I should cut off the nobles for their lands;
Desire his jewels, and this other's house.
The king-becoming graces,
I have no relish of them; but abound
In the division of each several crime
Acting it many ways.

**Macduff:**  O Scotland! Scotland!

**Malcolm:**  If such a one be fit to govern, speak:
I am as I have spoken.

**Macduff:**  Fit to govern?
No, not to live. O nation miserable,
With an untitled tyrant bloody-scepter'd,
When shalt thou see thy wholesome days again?

**Malcolm:**  Macduff, this noble passion,
Child of my integrity, hath from my soul
Wip'd the black scruples, reconcil'd my thoughts
To thy good truth and honour.

---

**Think about it**

Why does Malcolm have to test Macduff's
loyalty?

---

| **Act 4 Scene 3** | Ross tells Macduff what has happened to his family. Malcolm says they are ready to attack Macbeth. |
|---|---|

See who comes here.

What's the newest grief?

I have words that would be howl'd out in the desert air, where hearing should not latch them . . .

. . . the main part pertains to you alone.

If it be mine, keep it not from me.

Your castle is surpris'd; your wife and babes savagely slaughter'd.

My children too? My wife kill'd too?

I have said.

He has no children.

Dispute it like a man.

I shall do so; but I must also feel it as a man.

Front to front, bring thou this fiend of Scotland and myself.

Come, go we to the King. Macbeth is ripe for shaking.

<table>
<tr><td>**Act 5<br>Scene 1**</td><td>Lady Macbeth sleepwalks and goes over the bad things she and her husband have done. A doctor and her Gentlewoman (servant) watch and listen.</td><td></td></tr>
</table>

**Gentlewoman:** Lo you! here she comes.

**Doctor:** How came she by that light?

**Gentlewoman:** She has light by her continually; 'tis her command.

**Doctor:** You see, her eyes are open.

**Gentlewoman:** Ay, but their sense is shut.

**Doctor:** Look, how she rubs her hands.

**Gentlewoman:** It is an accustom'd action with her, to seem thus washing her hands. I have known her continue in this a quarter of an hour.

**Lady Macbeth:** Yet here's a spot.

**Doctor:** Hark! She speaks. I will set down what comes from her, to satisfy my remembrance the more strongly.

**Lady Macbeth:** Out, damned spot! Out, I say! One, two: why, then, 'tis time to do't. Hell is **murky**! Fie, my Lord,    dark
fie! A soldier and afeard? What need we fear who knows it, when none can call our power to **accompt**? Yet who would    account
have thought the old man to have had so much blood in him?

**Doctor:** Do you mark that?

**Lady Macbeth:** The Thane of Fife had a wife: where is she now? What, will these hands ne'er be clean? No more o'that, my Lord, no more o'that: you **mar** all with this starting.    spoil

**Doctor:** Go to, go to: you have known what you should not.

**Gentlewoman:** She has spoke what she should not, I am sure of that: Heaven knows what she has known.

**Lady Macbeth:** Here's the smell of blood still: all the perfumes of Arabia will not sweeten this little hand.

**Doctor:** This disease is beyond my practice. Yet I have known those which have walk'd in their sleep, who have died holily in their beds.

**Lady Macbeth:** Wash your hands, put on your night-gown; look not so pale. I tell you yet again, Banquo's buried: he cannot come out on's grave.

**Doctor:** Even so?

**Lady Macbeth:** To bed, to bed: there's knocking at the gate. Come, come, come, come, give me your hand. What's done cannot be undone.

**Doctor:** Will she go now to bed?

**Gentlewoman:** Directly.

**Doctor:** Foul whisp'rings are abroad. Unnatural deeds
Do breed unnatural troubles; infected minds
To their deaf pillows will discharge their secrets.
More needs she the divine than the physician.
Look after her;
Remove from her the means of all annoyance.

---

### Think about it

What does the last line tell you Lady Macbeth might do?

---

Two armies are marching to attack Macbeth. Malcolm leads the English soldiers. Here, some Scottish nobles with their troops discuss their plans.

The English power is near, led by Malcolm, his uncle Siward, and the good Macduff.

Near Birnam wood shall we meet them.

What does the tyrant?

Great Dunsinane he strongly fortifies. Some say he's mad; others, that lesser hate him, do call it valiant fury.

Now does he feel his secret murders sticking on his hands. Those he commands move only in command, nothing in love; now does he feel his title hang loose about him, like a giant's robe upon a dwarfish thief.

Make we our march towards Birnam.

The news reaching Macbeth is all bad for him. He is now desperate, but he still believes what the Witches and their spirits told him.

Bring me no more reports; let them fly all: till Birnam wood remove to Dunsinane, I cannot taint with fear.

What's the boy Malcolm? Was he not born of woman?

There is ten thousand.

Geese, villain?

Soldiers, Sir. The English force.

Take thy face hence.

I have liv'd long enough: my way of life is fall'n into the **sere**, the yellow leaf.

Seyton! I'll fight, till from my bones my flesh be hack'd. Give me my armour.

'Tis not needed yet.

I'll put it on.

**sere** – dry/parched

**physic** – medicine    **fly from me** – desert me    **bane** – ruin

Malcolm has reached Birnam wood which is close to Macbeth's castle at Dunsinane.

What wood is this before us?

The wood of Birnam.

Let every soldier hew him down a bough, and bear't before him: thereby shall we shadow the numbers of our host.

The confident tyrant keeps still in Dunsinane.

'Tis his main hope.

None serve him but **constrain'd things**.

### Think about it

What did the Witches' spirits say about Birnam wood?

**constrain'd things** – those who are forced to serve him

**Macbeth:** What is that noise?

**Seyton:** It is the cry of women, my good Lord.

[*He goes to investigate*]

**Macbeth:** I have almost forgot the taste of fears.
The time has been, my senses would have cool'd
To hear a night-shriek; and my fell of hair
Would at a **dismal treatise** rouse, and stir,    horror story
As life were in't. I have supp'd full with horrors;
**Direness**, familiar to my slaughterous thoughts,    evil
Cannot once start me.

[*Seyton returns*]

Wherefore was that cry?

**Seyton:** The Queen, my Lord, is dead.

**Macbeth:** She should have died hereafter;
There would have been a time for such a word.
To-morrow, and to-morrow, and to-morrow,
Creeps in this petty pace from day to day,
To the last syllable of recorded time;
And all our yesterdays have lighted fools
The way to dusty death. Out, out, brief candle!
Life's but a walking shadow; a poor player
That struts and frets his hour upon the stage,
And then is heard no more; it is a tale
Told by an idiot, full of sound and fury,
Signifying nothing.

[*A messenger comes in*]

Thou com'st to use thy tongue; thy story quickly.

**Messenger:** I should report that which I say I saw,
But know not how to do't.

**Macbeth:** Well, say, sir.

49

**Messenger:** As I did stand my watch upon the hill,
I look'd toward Birnam, and anon, methought,
The wood began to move.

**Macbeth:** Liar and slave!

**Messenger:** Let me endure your **wrath** if't be not so.    anger
Within this three mile may you see it coming:
I say, a moving grove.

**Macbeth:** If thou speak'st false,
Upon the next tree shalt thou hang alive,
Till famine cling thee; if thy speech be **sooth**,    true
I care not if thou dost for me as much.
I pull in resolution; and begin
To doubt th'**equivocation** of the fiend,    double meaning
That lies like truth: 'Fear not, till Birnam wood
Do come to Dunsinane'; and now a wood
Comes towards Dunsinane. Arm, arm, and out!
If this which he avouches does appear,
There is nor flying hence, nor **tarrying** here.    staying
I 'gin to be aweary of the sun,
And wish th'estate o' th' world were now undone.
Ring the alarum bell! Blow, wind! Come, wrack!
At least we'll die with **harness** on our back.    armour

---

### Think about it

What do you think Macbeth meant by 'She should have died hereafter'?

Would you say that Macbeth is still proud and brave?

The battle begins. Macbeth knows he cannot win, but he still believes he cannot be killed.

Now, near enough: your leafy screens throw down, and show like those you are.

Make all our trumpets speak.

They have tied me to a stake; I cannot fly, but bear-like, I must fight the course.

What is thy name?

Thou'lt be afraid to hear it.

No, though thou call'st thyself a hotter name than any is in hell.

Macbeth fights and kills Young Siward. Meanwhile, Macduff searches the battlefield for him and Macbeth's castle is captured.

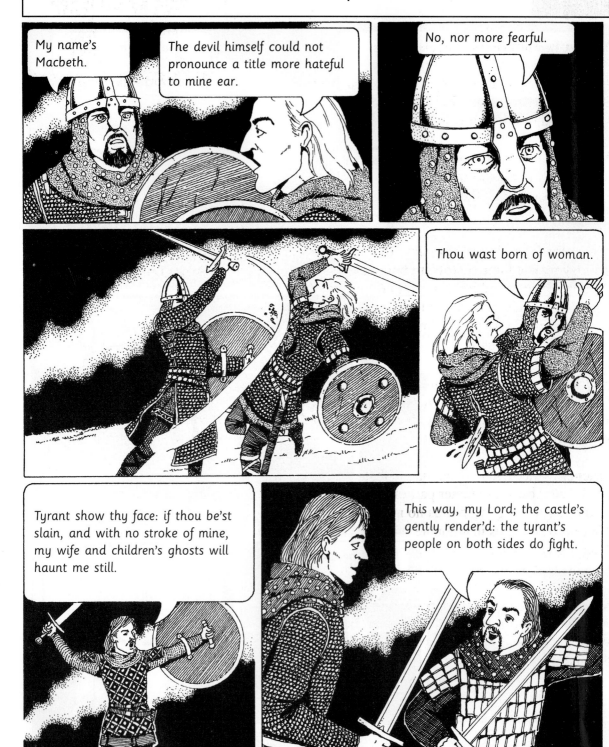

<table>
<tr><td>

**Act 5 °Scene 8**

</td><td>

Macduff finds Macbeth. They fight and . . .

</td><td>

</td></tr>
</table>

**Macduff:** Turn Hell-hound, turn!

**Macbeth:** Of all men else I have avoided thee:
But get thee back, my soul is too much charg'd
With blood of thine already.

**Macduff:** I have no words;
My voice is in my sword: thou bloodier villain
Than terms can give thee out!

                                  *[They start to fight]*

| | |
|---|---|
| **Macbeth: Thou losest labour**: | You're wasting energy |
| As easy may'st thou the **intrenchant** air | something that cannot be cut |
| With thy keen sword impress, as make me bleed: | |
| Let fall thy blade on vulnerable crests; | |
| I bear a charmed life; which must not yield | |
| To one of woman born. | |

| | |
|---|---|
| **Macduff:** Despair thy charm; | |
| And let the Angel, whom thou still hast serv'd, | |
| Tell thee, Macduff **was from his mother's womb** | born by caesarian section |
| **Untimely ripp'd**. | |

| | |
|---|---|
| **Macbeth:** Accursed be the tongue that tells me so, | |
| For it hath cow'd my better part of man: | |
| And be these **juggling fiends** no more believ'd, | the Witches |
| That **palter** with us in a double sense; | play |
| That keep the word of promise to our ear, | |
| And break it to our hope. I'll not fight with thee. | |

**Macduff:** Then yield thee, coward,
And live to be the show and gaze o' th' time:
We'll have thee, as our rarer monsters are,
Painted upon a pole, and underwrit,
'Here may you see the tyrant.'

**Macbeth:** I will not yield,
To kiss the ground before young Malcolm's feet,
And to be baited with the rabble's curse.
Though Birnam wood be come to Dunsinane,
And thou oppos'd, being of no woman born,
Yet I will try the last: before my body
I throw my warlike shield: lay on, Macduff;
And damn'd be him that first cries, 'Hold, enough!'

**Think about it**

What other prediction is now proved to have misled Macbeth?

Do you feel sorry for Macbeth at this stage?

The battle is over. Siward is told of his son's death. Macduff brings in Macbeth's head. Malcolm is greeted as King of Scotland.

**Had he his hurts before?** – Did he die facing the enemy?

Behold, where stands th'usurper's cursed head.

The time is free.

Hail, King of Scotland!

Hail, King of Scotland!

My Thanes and kinsmen, henceforth be earls.

What's more to do, as calling home our exil'd friends abroad that fled; producing forth the cruel ministers of this dead butcher and his fiend-like queen, who, as 'tis thought, by self and violent hands took off her life.

So thanks to all at once, and to each one, whom we invite to see us crown'd at Scone.

THE END

56

*Also available in this series:*

Twelfth Night
Twelfth Night – Teacher's Resource Book

Romeo and Juliet
Romeo and Juliet – Teacher's Resource Book

*Forthcoming (early 2000)*
Henry V
Henry V – Teacher's Resource Book